CHICAGO PUBLIC LIBRARY
SULZER REGIONAL
4455 N. LINCOLN AVE. 60625

REF
TF
25
.C554
C55
1997

SULZER

Chicago Public Library

R0 252831

Chicago, St. Pa   Minneapolis & Om

CHICAGO, ST. PAUL, MINNEAPOLIS & OMAHA RAILWAY 1880 - 1940

PHOTO ARCHIVE

D1604879

Iconografix continuously seeks collections of archival photographs for reproduction in future books. We require a minimum of 120 photographs per subject. We prefer subjects narrow in focus, i.e., a specific model, railroad, racing venue, etc. Photographs must be of high-quality, suited to reproduction in an 8x10-inch format. We willingly pay for the use of photographs.

If you own or know of such a collection, please contact: The Publisher, Iconografix, PO Box 609, Osceola, Wisconsin 54020.

CHICAGO, ST. PAUL, MINNEAPOLIS & OMAHA RAILWAY 1880 - 1940
PHOTO ARCHIVE

Photographs from
The State Historical Society of Wisconsin

Edited with introduction by
P. A. Letourneau

Iconografix
Photo Archive Series

Iconografix
PO Box 609
Osceola, Wisconsin 54020 USA

Text Copyright © 1997

All rights reserved. No part of this work may be reproduced or used in any form by any means... graphic, electronic, or mechanical, including photocopying, recording, taping, or any other information storage and retrieval system... without written permission of the publisher.

We acknowledge that certain words, such as model names and designations, mentioned herein are the property of the trademark holder. We use them for purposes of identification only. Information contained herein is true to the best of our knowledge. This is not an official publication.

Books in the Iconografix *Photo Archive Series* are offered at a discount when sold in quantity for promotional use. Businesses or organizations seeking details should write to the Marketing Department, Iconografix, at the above address.

Library of Congress Card Number 96-78344

ISBN 1-882256-67-0

97 98 99 00 01 02 03 5 4 3 2 1

Printed in the United States of America

Cover Photo: A Chicago, St. Paul, Minneapolis & Omaha passenger train ready to leave Union Depot, St. Paul, Minnesota, 1883.

R01272 52881

PREFACE

The histories of machines and mechanical gadgets are contained in the books, journals, correspondence, and personal papers stored in libraries and archives throughout the world. Written in tens of languages, covering thousands of subjects, the stories are recorded in millions of words.

Words are powerful. Yet, the impact of a single image, a photograph or an illustration, often relates more than dozens of pages of text. Fortunately, many of the libraries and archives that house the words also preserve the images.

In the *Photo Archive Series*, Iconografix reproduces photographs and illustrations selected from public and private collections. The images are chosen to tell a story—to capture the character of their subject. Reproduced as found, they are accompanied by the captions made available by the archive.

The Iconografix *Photo Archive Series* is dedicated to young and old alike, the enthusiast, the collector and anyone who, like us, is fascinated by "things" mechanical.

CHICAGO PUBLIC LIBRARY
SULZER REGIONAL
4455 N. LINCOLN AVE. 60625

The enginehouse and wood-burning engines of the West Wisconsin Railway Company, circa 1878. The West Wisconsin was the principal predecessor line of the Chicago, St. Paul, Minneapolis & Omaha Railway.

INTRODUCTION

The Chicago, St. Paul, Minneapolis and Omaha Railway Company, hereinafter referred to as the "Omaha Co." or the "Omaha," was incorporated in May 1880. It was created by the consolidation of the Chicago, St. Paul and Minneapolis Railway Company (successor in interest to the West Wisconsin Railway Company) and the North Wisconsin Railway Company. Subsequently, in 1881, the company completed the purchase of the St. Paul and Sioux City Railroad Company, thus forming the foundation upon which the Omaha was built. Over a long period of years, the Omaha Co. evolved through a series of constructions, consolidations, and mergers and purchases of various railroads under some 40 or more corporate names.

The Omaha Co. was itself the subject of purchase at a very early point in its history. In November 1882, the majority of its capital stock was purchased by the Chicago and North Western Railway Company (C&NW). Ironically, the Omaha came into existence only because the Chicago and North Western had earlier declined to purchase the West Wisconsin Railway. In 1875, the West Wisconsin came under the control of Henry H. Porter, who was also a director of the C&NW. Porter later wrote that he had believed ownership of the West Wisconsin "would be greatly to the advantage of the Chicago and North Western Railway." Consequently, immediately after Porter and two partners purchased the railroad, they tendered it to the C&NW. However, Porter's fellow C&NW directors saw no advantage to his offer and declined it.

Finding themselves the owners of a railroad (and about 190 miles of track), Porter and his partners set about to expand it. Under Porter's direction, the West Wisconsin Railway Company was reorganized as the Chicago, St. Paul and Minneapolis Railway Company. The partners soon gained control of the North Wisconsin Railway. Integration of the St. Paul and Sioux City Railroad came next. Although not completed before May 1881, consent to purchase or consolidate with the St. Paul and Sioux City was provided for within the very articles of consolidation that created the Omaha.

At the time of its formation, the Omaha Co. owned less than 300 miles of road, all of which was located in Wisconsin as its operations in Minnesota were conducted over leased trackage. Further growth followed construction of new lines and expansion of the existing lines, such that by December 31, 1881 the Omaha Co. owned 979.32 miles of road. In addition to the expanded and newly built lines, in 1881 the Omaha Co. spent in excess of $1.5 million for permanent improvements, including: a new General Office Building in St. Paul; $31,000 for new transfer steamers at the Missouri River at Sioux City, Iowa; valuable depot and transfer grounds at Minneapolis; extensive improvements at St. Paul Shops; and rebuilding bridges across the Eau Claire, Chippewa, and St. Croix Rivers in Wisconsin. Equipment acquired included 20 locomotives, 15 passenger cars, and 634 freight cars. Additional orders were placed for 200 box cars, 350 flat cars, 25 locomotives, and seven passenger cars. Earnings in 1881 were reported at $3,994,319. Another $3.5 million was spent in 1882 for new equipment, improvements, and construction. Expansion of the line was such that, by the time the Chicago and North Western acquired it, the Omaha owned some 1,300 miles of track.

The Omaha Co. was operated independently of the C&NW, from its own headquarters in St. Paul, Minnesota. (It was 1957 before the Chicago, St. Paul, Minneapolis & Omaha was fully absorbed into the Chicago & North Western.) As such, its history, as preserved in the papers of Carl R. Gray Jr., in 1937 Executive Vice President and General Manager of the Omaha, and in the photographs Gray collected and donated to the State Historical Society of Wisconsin, is extensive and well-documented.

The focus of this book is on the equipment and operations of the Chicago, St. Paul, Minneapolis & Omaha Railway in the years from 1880 to 1940, the period covered most thoroughly by the Gray Collection. In this brief introduction, it is only possible to relate the highlights of the Omaha's history. Much of the story is conveyed through the photographs and captions. The photographs are organized in near chronological order, with dates cited if known. Very often, however, the only certain date is that when a particular locomotive was built or placed in service, or the date a particular structure was built. In such cases, that is the date cited, and the photograph may, therefore, appear out of sequence. Certain photographs are not from the Gray Collection, and may have been taken after 1940. Photographs of locomotives from the predecessor railroads, i.e., the Minnesota Valley Railroad and West Wisconsin Railway, are included either for their historical value or because the engines continued in service following the formation of the Omaha Co. Now, back to the story!

The Omaha was originally organized into five divisions: Northern Division; Eastern Division (Elroy, Wisconsin to St. Paul); St. Paul Division (St. Paul to St. James, Minnesota); Sioux City Division (St. James to Sioux City, Iowa); and the Nebraska Division. Between 1883 and 1890, the major historical highlights included construction of a line from Eau Claire, Wisconsin to Chippewa Falls, which further united the Eastern and Northern Divisions (1883). Yard, tracks, depot, enginehouse, turntable were established at Northern Division headquarters in Spooner (1883). The Omaha joined with eight other railroads to form the Minnesota Transfer Railway, the primary transfer line within and around the Minneapolis-St. Paul area (1883). The St. Paul Division and the Sioux City Division were consolidated as the St. Paul and Sioux City Division, and seated in St. James (1883), and were later moved to offices in the new depot in Mankato, Minnesota (1885). Trackage furnishing entrance to and terminal facilities in Duluth, Minnesota was put into operation (1886). Extension of the Sioux Falls (South Dakota) Line to Mitchell, South Dakota (1887). Opening of the Sioux City Bridge (1888) eliminated the need to transfer freight cars across the Missouri River by ferry in summer and temporary bridge in winter. Extensive improvement and expansion of car shops at Hudson, Wisconsin (1890).

Historical highlights for the period 1891 to 1900 included acquisition of the Sault Ste. Marie & Southwestern Railway (1891). Movement of headquarters of the Northern Division from Spooner to Itasca, Wisconsin (1896). The Omaha Co. reported earnings of $8.15 million (1896). Headquarters of the St. Paul and Sioux City Division were returned to St. James (1898). The main line and branches formerly known as the St. Paul and Sioux City Division were designated as the Minnesota and Iowa Division, and the Northern and Eastern Divisions were consolidated and designated as the Wisconsin Division (1900).

At the turn of the 20th century, the Omaha operated over approximately 1,492 miles, divided as follows: Wisconsin Division, 661 miles; St. Paul and Sioux City Division, 553 miles; Nebraska Division, 278 miles. It connected with the C&NW at 17 different points. Although the Omaha had not grown significantly in miles of trackage operated, many improvements had been made since 1882—including the purchase of numerous locomotives and other rolling stock—so that its continued prosperity as a vital part of The North-Western Line seemed assured.

Historical highlights for the years 1901 to 1915 included transfer of Wisconsin Division Headquarters from St. Paul to Eau Claire (1905). Adoption of an employee pension plan (1906). Work was begun and completed on a second track, beginning in Merrillan (1906) and completed at Northline (1913). Installation of automatic electric safety signals between the Twin Cities and Elroy, Wisconsin (1911-1915). Separation of the Eastern and Northern Districts of the Wisconsin Division into separate divisions, with headquarters at Eau Claire and Spooner, respectively (1912). The extension of the line to Park Falls, Wisconsin (1914), which constituted the final episode in construction of additional branch lines. Thus, in June 1914, the initial 22 miles of road constructed in 1865 by the Minnesota Valley Railroad Company had expanded to a point where the Omaha Co., as its successor in interest, owned and operated 1,866.25 miles of railroad in five states.

Historical highlights for the years 1916 to 1934 included construction of a new eight-story General Office Building in St. Paul (1917). Federal control of the US railroad and transportation systems, including the Omaha (1917-1920). Consolidation of the Eastern and Northern Divisions at Eau Claire (1925). Delivery of the last new steam locomotives (1930). Oiling of the roadbed (1931-1935).

Dissolution of the Nebraska Division with control of its operations assumed by the Western Division (1933).

Historical highlights for the years 1935 to 1940 included creation of the Head of the Lakes Terminal Division (1935). Mileage operated on the Omaha Main Line was 1,652.29 miles and all tracks was 2,544.94 miles (1935). Operating revenues of $15.45 million (1935).

Arguably, the most significant event of the final six year period in this history of the Omaha was the inauguration, on January 2, 1935 by the Chicago and North Western, of a "fast train" between Minneapolis and Chicago. The "400" derived its name from the expression "400 miles in less than 400 minutes." This was, according to its operators, "the fastest schedule ever operated up to that time between (the two cities)." The boost in prestige had an overall positive impact across the North Western Line. In 1935, the Omaha reported an 11.4% increase in passenger revenue, the first year to show a gain since 1923. The arrival of the fast train brought with it the advent of streamlining and the use of alloy steel in train construction. By 1939 the original 400, which consisted of standard-size steel passenger cars pulled by oil-burning steam locomotives, was replaced by "The Amazing New 400," two complete new trains of special design, light-weight alloy construction, streamlined, and, most significantly, diesel-powered. The days of steam were numbered. The arrival of the Omaha's first two diesel locomotives followed in October 1940. These two switchers, No. 55, an EMC 600 horsepower unit, and No. 90, an Alco-GE 1000 horsepower unit, marked the beginning of the diesel era for the Chicago, St. Paul, Minneapolis & Omaha Railway, and bring an end to our review of the Omaha.

9

The Shakopee, a combination locomotive and coach built in 1865, served the Minnesota Valley Railroad. Organized in 1864, Minnesota Valley was the oldest predecessor line of the Chicago, St. Paul, Minneapolis & Omaha Railway.

No. 219, the former *Belle Plaine* of the St. Paul and Sioux City, built in 1866 and retired in 1899.

Engines #8 and #9 of the St. Paul & Sioux City photographed at St. Peter, Minnesota in 1870. Renumbered 208 and 209, respectively, the former was rebuilt as a 0-4-0 from a 4-4-0 in 1886, and was retired in 1909. No. 209 was sold to a dealer in 1899.

West Wisconsin #21, *T.C. Pound,* was a Baldwin 4-4-0 that entered service in October 1872 and was retired by the Omaha in January 1901.

Engine #18, a Baldwin-built 4-6-0, entered service on the West Wisconsin in 1872 and was retired by the Omaha in 1909.

This portrait of 1872 features locomotive #12, *Geo. W. Clinton*, of the West Wisconsin Railway posed in front of the Hudson, Wisconsin station. The general offices of the railroad were upstairs in the station, which opened in 1871. At the far right of the lineup of dignitaries was D.A. Baldwin, president of the railroad. No. 12, a Baldwin 4-4-0 built in 1871, served the Omaha until it was sold in 1898.

St. Paul's Union Depot soon after it opened in 1880. The Omaha was one of eight shareholders in the St. Paul Union Depot Company, that among others included the Great Northern, the Northern Pacific, and the Chicago, Milwaukee, St. Paul & Pacific.

A train led by locomotive #13, *L.J. Foley,* of the former West Wisconsin Railway. This class B-1 Baldwin 4-4-0 was built in 1871 and served the Omaha until it was sold to F.M. Hicks, a Chicago dealer, in 1899. This circa 1880 photograph captured the train west of Niellsville, Wisconsin, in the vicinity of Black River Falls.

A group of hunters posed with their kill. No. 55, a Baldwin class D-5 4-4-0, served the Omaha from 1881 to 1916.

One of the Omaha's first baggage cars, circa 1881.

Engine #229, formerly the *Geo. A. Hamilton* of the Sioux City & St. Paul, with the pay car in tow. Built by Taunton in 1872, this class A-2 4-4-0 was sold to E.H. Hobe Lumber Co. in 1900.

This Omaha pay car was in use until 1893.

The first cars of an Omaha-bound special train of 24 "Lumber-Line" cars, each 35 feet long and loaded with lumber products from the Eau Claire Lumber Company. Photographed at Eau Claire, Wisconsin on September 1, 1882.

Engine #116 and a construction crew near St. Peter, Minnesota. No. 116 was one of ten 4-4-0 class E-5s delivered from Rhode Island in late 1882. It was retired in September 1916.

The Elmore, Minnesota station played host to a train led by engine #86, a class D-6 4-4-0 delivered from Baldwin in 1883.

Another view of the Elmore station, located just north of the Minnesota-Iowa border.

The Chicago, St. Paul, Minneapolis & Omaha Railway General Office Building in 1883, decorated in honor of the celebration of the opening of the Northern Pacific Railroad to the West Coast. The building was renovated in 1889 following a fire, at which time a fourth floor was added. In 1916 it was razed and a new building was constructed.

Engine #23, built by Baldwin, entered service on the West Wisconsin in 1872. Photographed in 1884, it was retired by the Omaha in August 1901.

This engine and caboose were in train service at Montrose, South Dakota in the summer of 1884, after which the engine hauled gravel from the Montrose pit for patching road between Hartford and Salem, South Dakota.

The Ashland, Wisconsin facility in July 1886. Built by the Ashland Railway Company, in the interest of the Omaha, the road served Ashland to Bayfield, Wisconsin along the so-called "Bay Front Tracks." The railroad and its properties were conveyed to the Omaha in December 1885.

Engine #247 at Sioux City in 1888 and shortly before it was sold. This 3-foot 6-inch gauge 0-6-0, built by Mason in 1876, was acquired by the St. Paul and Sioux City Railroad in 1880 through the foreclosure sale of the Covington, Columbus & Black Hills Railroad. The engine, as shown, was equipped for handling cars in Missouri River ferry boat service prior to construction of the Sioux City Bridge in 1888.

Engine #154, on the point of a Nebraska Division passenger train, at the east end of the Sioux City Bridge. The locomotive, a class E-7 4-4-0 from Schenectady, entered service in June 1888 and was retired in March 1927. The Sioux City Bridge, opened to traffic in November 1888, spanned the Missouri River, and was a joint project of the Omaha Co. and the Chicago and North Western.

Engine #156, one of six class E-7 Schenectady 4-4-0s added to the Omaha roster in June 1888, photographed at the St. James, Minnesota depot. This unit was retired from service in March 1927.

Locomotive #57 at Spooner, Wisconsin in 1888. This Baldwin class D-5 4-4-0 entered service in October 1888, and was retired in September 1913. Spooner was an important point on the Omaha. In 1893 it was made the seat of the Northern Division.

Locomotive #171, delivered from Schenectady in 1888, was not retired before 1935. A noteworthy 47 years of service.

Engine #249, a Hinkley 4-4-0 and formerly engine #1 of the Omaha & Northwestern Railroad, photographed in 1890 in service on the "Bonnie Doon" branch, between Luverne, Minnesota and Doon, Iowa.

Engine #184, previously of the Winona & St. Peter and the C&NW, a class B-1 4-4-0 built by Hinkley in 1885 and acquired by the Omaha in 1890. Photographed between Tunnel and Elroy, Wisconsin sometime in the 1890s. This engine was retired in February 1909.

A way-freight at Rice Lake, Wisconsin, circa 1890.

Engine #214 equipped for yard service at 7th and Howard Streets, Sioux City, Iowa, circa 1890. An ex-North Wisconsin Railway 4-4-0 built by Taunton in 1872, it was sold to the Jump River Lumber Co. in 1899.

Engine #36, a Baldwin 0-4-0 that entered Chicago, St. Paul and Minneapolis service in 1879 and was sold to a dealer in 1899.

Collisions were once a more frequent tragedy of railroading. This accident between two C.St.P.M.&O. trains occurred near Tramway, Wisconsin in 1891.

Engr. Jos. Sandy, in cab; Fireman Harry Wood, on running board.

No. 174, a class E-9 4-6-0, one of six delivered from Schenectady in April 1891.

A floral arrangement at the funeral of an Omaha engineer, St. Paul, 1891.

Engine #214, as it appeared in 1892. This Baldwin 2-8-0 consolidation was used in transfer service by the Omaha from May 1890 until it was retired in 1928.

A special flour train departing the Pillsbury Mills for Omaha on January 29, 1892.

No. 265, a ten-wheeler delivered from Schenectady in July 1892 and retired in July 1928.

Engine #7 captured in 1894 at Marshfield, Wisconsin. This Baldwin 4-4-0 entered service only months before the consolidation that created the Omaha, and it was retired by 1917.

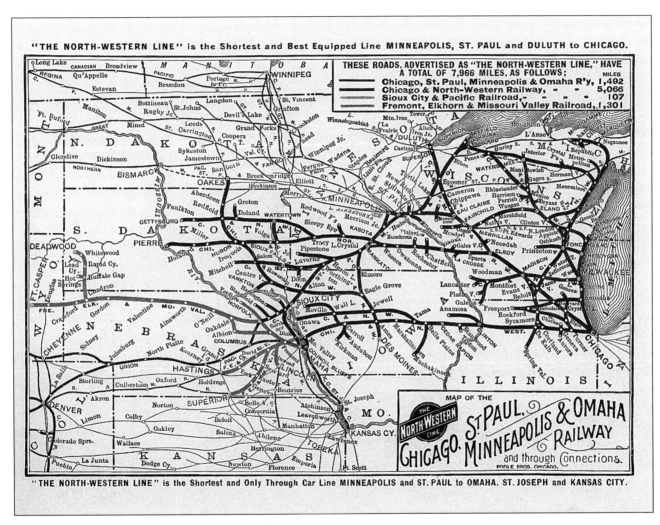

This route map of 1895 touted the qualities of the NORTH-WESTERN LINE and conveyed the significant position played in the system by the Chicago, St. Paul, Minneapolis & Omaha Railway.

The Luverne, Minnesota depot, circa 1895.

Engine #158, a class E-7 Schenectady 4-4-0, posed with engineers
William H. Neal and "Jink" Jinkin Moore, circa 1898.

Engine #257, one of seven Schenectady class F-8 4-4-0s delivered in 1898. No. 257 remained on the Omaha roster until January 1940.

Train #18, led by locomotive #100, as this fast freight moved
through the Minnesota countryside at 10:51 A.M., July 23, 1898.

The incredible aftermath of a rear end collision between two extra freight trains, where three engines and 22 cars of grain went down with the bridge into the Des Moines River at Windom, Minnesota.

No. 255, another one of seven Schenectady class F-8 4-4-0s delivered in 1898. No. 255 was retired in 1933.

An Omaha sleeping car arranged for daytime travel, circa late 1890s.

No. 283, a Schenectady 4-6-0 class F-9 and one of ten delivered in 1898.

SCENE IN DAY PARLOR CAR,
ON "THE NORTH-WESTERN LINE."

An Omaha day parlor car, circa 1900.

56

No. 209, a Baldwin 2-8-0 class H-2 delivered in October 1898.

This circa 1900 photograph is identified merely as the St. Paul Yards. Note the workmen and horse-drawn wagon.

A bridge crew at work on Bridge 78 across the Eau Galle River at Spring Valley, Wisconsin. Engine #58 was a class D-5 4-4-0 built by Baldwin. It entered service in October 1881 and was retired in June 1922.

A fairly typical small town depot, circa 1900, this one at Turtle Lake, Wisconsin, south of Spooner.

The Minneapolis Paint Shop crew in 1900.

Car #97, circa 1900.

A circa 1900 photo of decking logs somewhere in Wisconsin, while C.St.P.M&O. cars wait at the siding.

No. 85 on the point of a passenger train on the Elmore line, 1900. This Baldwin 4-4-0 served the Omaha from 1883 to 1917.

No. 186 at St. James, Minnesota in 1901. This class D-11 0-6-0 was delivered from Schenectady in 1892. It remained in service until it was retired in 1927.

A work train operating a rail unloader on loan from the C&NW, 1901.

Sunday in camp. The extra gang at Cumberland, Wisconsin, 1901.

Engine #255 decorated to handle employees on a run to Prior Lake, Minnesota, June 22, 1901, for the 16th annual shop picnic.

No. 330, delivered from the Alco-Schnectady Works in 1903.

The Chandler Gravel Pit loading crew and engine #221, Pequot, Minnesota, 1903.

No. 371, delivered from Schenectady in 1903, was the first 4-6-2 Pacific to serve the Omaha.

A crew headed to Chandler Pit, 1903. Engine #287 was one of ten class F-9 ten-wheelers delivered from Schenectady in 1898. It was retired in May 1935.

No. 374, one of the five class I-2 Pacifics delivered from Schenectady in 1903.

Locomotive #136 leads a fast-time freight, somewhere on the Nebraska Division, 1903.

No. 375, one of the five class I-2 Pacifics delivered from Schenectady in 1903. All five remained in service until 1937.

A group of union delegates from Spooner posed in front of the engine of a special train that carried them to St. Paul in 1904 for the first union meeting.

ST. PAUL SHOPS 1904
1 - H.A. KARSTADT
2 - JACK HENDERSON
3 - HARRY SMITH
4 - THOS. LEITH
5 - JAKE BLECKLEY
6 - EMIL MATAK
7 - JOS. SVOBODNY
8 - JOHN GORGOSCHLITZ
9 - WM. SASSOR
10 - HEBERT JOHNSON

St. Paul Tank Shop employees, 1904.

Blizzards were just one type of natural disaster that could disrupt service on the Omaha. A snow crew paused in Windom, Minnesota during the winter of 1904.

Flooding brought a halt to this Omaha train at Ponca, Nebraska, circa 1905.

The Duluth city ticket office, 1905.

A 1905 "Day-tripper" on the Chippewa Bridge at Eau Claire, Wisconsin.

Construction work on the Sioux City Shops, 1905.

No. 216, class H-2 2-8-0 consolidation, delivered from Alco-Schenectady in 1905. It was scrapped in 1949.

The Emerson, Nebraska station, circa 1905.

No. 370, one of seven class G-3 Atlantics from Alco-Schenectady delivered in 1905 and 1906. All seven were retired in 1950.

Engine #266, circa 1907, a class F-5 Schenectady 4-6-0 that entered service in July 1892 and was retired in December 1928.

The Altoona, Wisconsin Roundhouse crew in 1907. The man at the top of the photograph was E.W. Puhl, a visiting former Omaha brakeman turned magician, who assumed the stagename "Marco".

X.O., a saddle back tank engine converted in 1907 from former engine #152. Until it was retired in 1916, X.O. was used for handling engines at the St. Paul Shops.

Bridge work at an unidentified location, circa 1910.

Locomotive #176 at Pender, Nebraska in 1908. No. 176, a class E-9 4-6-0 delivered from Schenectady in 1891, was retired in late 1928.

The 1910 wreck of a train led by engine #371 near Fairchild, Wisconsin. No. 371, the Omaha's first 4-6-2 Pacific, appears in a better state on page 71.

The second #36 on the Omaha, a class M-1 0-6-0 from Alco introduced into service in 1911 and sold in 1935.

No. 112, a class K-1 4-6-0 delivered from Alco-Schenectady in 1911.

No. 230, another class K-1 4-6-0 delivered from Alco-Schenectady in 1911.

No. 388, a class K-2 4-6-2 delivered from Alco-Schenectady in 1911.

The Minneapolis city ticket office in 1912.

No. 235, a class K-1 4-6-0 delivered from Alco-Brooks Works in 1912.

A Lidgerwood Gravel Unloader at work on the line in 1912.

A Jordan Spreader at work on the line in 1912.

No. 244, another class K-1 4-6-0 delivered from Alco-Brooks Works in 1912.

No. 110, a class K-1 4-6-0 delivered from Alco-Schenectady in 1913.

No. 506, a class E Pacific delivered from Alco-Schenectady in 1913, on the point of a passenger train.

No. 395, a class J 2-8-2 delivered from Alco-Schenectady in 1913.

No. 184, a class K-1 4-6-0 delivered from Alco-Schenectady in 1913.

A crew taking out the old line bridge at Black River Falls, Wisconsin in 1914.

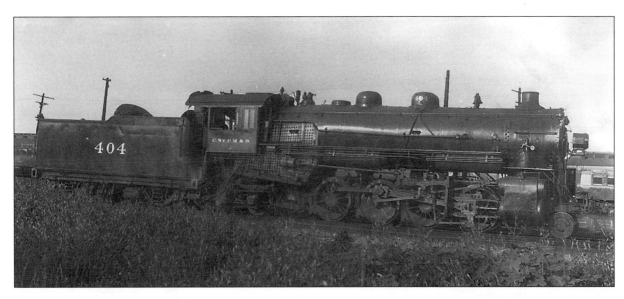

No. 404 at the Minneapolis enginehouse. A class J 2-8-2 Mikado delivered from Alco-Schenectady Works in April 1914, it was later rebuilt to a class J-a.

No. 363 at Fairchild, Wisconsin, 1914.

The Hudson, Wisconsin Hand Car
Shop was built in 1916.

The Hudson, Wisconsin Machine
Shop was built in 1916.

No. 512, a 4-6-2 class E Pacific delivered from Alco-Schenectady in January 1916.

No. 407, another class-J 2-8-2 Mikado (later rebuilt to class J-a) delivered from Alco-Schenectady Works in 1916.

Omaha employees posed with the mock armoured tank built for the 1917 Liberty Loan Drive. The smoke from the machine guns was the units gas engine exhaust.

The Wheel Shop, Hudson Wisconsin, circa 1920.

Locomotive #426, a class J-2 Mikado, delivered from Alco-Richmond Works in January 1921.

No. 437, a class J-3 2-8-2 Mikado, delivered from Alco-Schenectady, in November 1926.

No. 439, a class J-3 2-8-2 Mikado, delivered from Alco-Schenectady, in November 1926.

No. 602, a Pacific class E-3 4-6-2 delivered in November 1930.

Another view of #602 in service. No. 602 was the last steam locomotive purchased by the Omaha, one of three Pacifics delivered in 1930.

The St. Paul Machine Shop crew, 1930.

Two "Stott Briquet" specials loaded for a trip west, May 27, 1931.

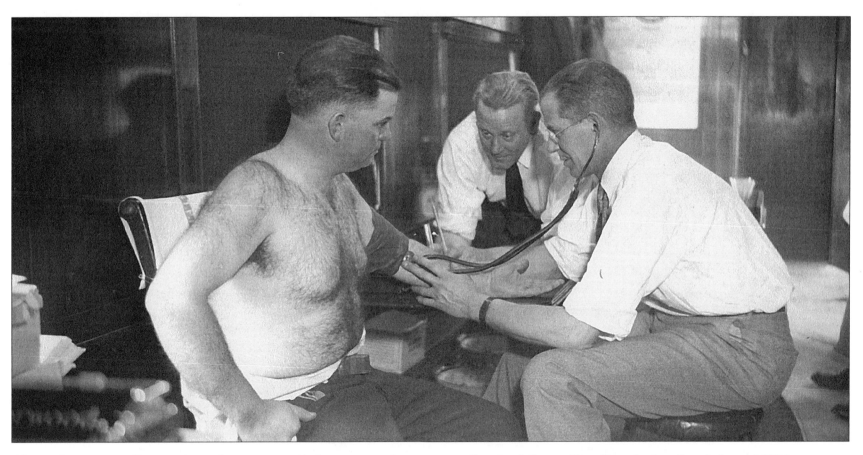

Aboard a specially equipped car, a switchman undergoes a physical from the Omaha's physician, 1934.

A rail renewal gang at work on an unidentified stretch of the Omaha, July 1936.

Members of the rail removal gang operate a spike puller.

No. 413, one of ten 2-8-2 Mikados delivered from Alco-Schenectady Works in October 1916, as it emerged from the St. Paul Shop in September 1937.

Diesel-power comes to the Omaha. No. 90, an Alco-GE 1000 horsepower diesel, was one of two diesel locomotives delivered in October 1940.

Photo Credits

The majority of photographs in this book are from the collection of the State Historical Society of Wisconsin, and are reproduced with their permission. The images for which the Society maintains a negative are cited by page and negative catalog number below:

Page 6 (X3) 34845, State Historical Society of Wisconsin; **Page 12** (X3) 33296, State Historical Society of Wisconsin; **Page 13** (X3) 35203, State Historical Society of Wisconsin; **Page 14** (X3) 38690, State Historical Society of Wisconsin; **Page 15** (X3) 34954, State Historical Society of Wisconsin; **Page 16** (X3) 39149, State Historical Society of Wisconsin; **Page 17** (X3) 7893, State Historical Society of Wisconsin; **Page 18** (X3i) 3946, State Historical Society of Wisconsin; **Page 22** (X3) 13471, State Historical Society of Wisconsin; **Page 26** (X3) 48454, State Historical Society of Wisconsin; **Page 27** (X3) 28974, State Historical Society of Wisconsin; **Page 29** (X3) 27258, State Historical Society of Wisconsin; **Page 30** (X3) 40169, State Historical Society of Wisconsin; **Page 33** (X3) 34955, State Historical Society of Wisconsin; **Page 35** (X3) 38689, State Historical Society of Wisconsin; **Page 36** (X3) 18780, State Historical Society of Wisconsin; **Page 37** (X3) 24765, State Historical Society of Wisconsin; **Page 38** (X3) 38691, State Historical Society of Wisconsin; **Page 39** (W6) 19632, State Historical Society of Wisconsin; **Page 40** (X3) 47277, State Historical Society of Wisconsin; **Page 41** (X3) 46997, State Historical Society of Wisconsin; **Page 43** (X3) 46434, State Historical Society of Wisconsin; **Page 48** (X3) 46999, State Historical Society of Wisconsin; **Page 54** (X3) 23912, State Historical Society of Wisconsin; **Page 56** (X3) 14821, State Historical Society of Wisconsin; **Page 60** (X3) 27259, State Historical Society of Wisconsin; **Page 64** (X3) 32850, State Historical Society of Wisconsin; **Page 65** (X3) 46996, State Historical Society of Wisconsin; **Page 70** (X3) 39152, State Historical Society of Wisconsin; **Page 72** (X3) 39263, State Historical Society of Wisconsin; **Page 76** (X3) 39150, State Historical Society of Wisconsin; **Page 80** (X3) 50840, State Historical Society of Wisconsin; **Page 86** (X3) 47278, State Historical Society of Wisconsin; **Page 88** (X3) 32854, State Historical Society of Wisconsin

Certain photographs in this book arc from the collection of the Minnesota Historical Society, and are reproduced with their permission. The page and catalog reference numbers of those images are cited below:

Page 34 III.26.200, Minnesota Historical Society; **Page 50** III.26.199, Minnesota Historical Society; **Page 73** III.26.222, Minnesota Historical Society; **Page 96** III.26.196, Minnesota Historical Society; **Page 97** III.26.192, Minnesota Historical Society; **Page 99** III.26.184, Minnesota Historical Society; **Page 101** III.26.182, Minnesota Historical Society; **Page 102** III.26.183, Minnesota Historical Society; **Page 103** III.26.187, Minnesota Historical Society; **Page 105** III.26.203, Minnesota Historical Society; **Page 110** III.26.185, Minnesota Historical Society; **Page 111** III.26.186, Minnesota Historical Society; **Page 116** III.26.215, Minnesota Historical Society; **Page 118** III.26.212, Minnesota Historical Society

The Iconografix Photo Archive Series includes:

AMERICAN CULTURE

AMERICAN SERVICE STATIONS 1935-1943	ISBN 1-882256-27-1
COCA-COLA: A HISTORY IN PHOTOGRAPHS 1930-1969	ISBN 1-882256-46-8
COCA-COLA: ITS VEHICLES IN PHOTOGRAPHS 1930-1969	ISBN 1-882256-47-6
PHILLIPS 66 1945-1954	ISBN 1-882256-42-5

AUTOMOTIVE

IMPERIAL 1955-1963	ISBN 1-882256-22-0
IMPERIAL 1964-1968	ISBN 1-882256-23-9
LE MANS 1950: THE BRIGGS CUNNINGHAM CAMPAIGN	ISBN 1-882256-21-2
PACKARD MOTOR CARS 1935-1942	ISBN 1-882256-44-1
PACKARD MOTOR CARS 1946-1958	ISBN 1-882256-45-X
SEBRING 12-HOUR RACE 1970	ISBN 1-882256-20-4
STUDEBAKER 1933-1942	ISBN 1-882256-24-7
STUDEBAKER 1946-1958	ISBN 1-882256-25-5
LINCOLN MOTOR CARS 1920-1942	ISBN 1-882256-57-3
LINCOLN MOTOR CARS 1946-1960	ISBN 1-882256-58-1
MG 1945-1964	ISBN 1-882256-52-2
MG 1965-1980	ISBN 1-882256-53-0
GT40	ISBN 1-882256-64-6
FERRARI PININFARINA 1952-1996	ISBN 1-882256-65-4
VANDERBILT CUP RACE 1936 & 1937	ISBN 1-882256-66-2

TRACTORS AND CONSTRUCTION EQUIPMENT

CASE TRACTORS 1912-1959	ISBN 1-882256-32-8
CATERPILLAR MILITARY TRACTORS VOLUME 1	ISBN 1-882256-16-6
CATERPILLAR MILITARY TRACTORS VOLUME 2	ISBN 1-882256-17-4
CATERPILLAR SIXTY	ISBN 1-882256-05-0
CATERPILLAR THIRTY	ISBN 1-882256-04-2
CLETRAC AND OLIVER CRAWLERS	ISBN 1-882256-43-3
ERIE SHOVEL	ISBN 1-882256-69-7
FARMALL F- SERIES	ISBN 1-882256-02-6
FARMALL MODEL H	ISBN 1-882256-03-4
FARMALL MODEL M	ISBN 1-882256-15-8
FARMALL REGULAR	ISBN 1-882256-14-X
FARMALL SUPER SERIES	ISBN 1-882256-49-2

FORDSON 1917-1928	ISBN 1-882256-33-6
HART-PARR	ISBN 1-882256-08-5
HOLT TRACTORS	ISBN 1-882256-10-7
INTERNATIONAL TRACTRACTOR	ISBN 1-882256-48-4
JOHN DEERE MODEL A	ISBN 1-882256-12-3
JOHN DEERE MODEL B	ISBN 1-882256-01-8
JOHN DEERE MODEL D	ISBN 1-882256-00-X
JOHN DEERE 30 SERIES	ISBN 1-882256-13-1
MINNEAPOLIS-MOLINE U-SERIES	ISBN 1-882256-07-7
OLIVER TRACTORS	ISBN 1-882256-09-3
RUSSELL GRADERS	ISBN 1-882256-11-5
TWIN CITY TRACTOR	ISBN 1-882256-06-9

RAILWAYS

CHICAGO, ST. PAUL, MINNEAPOLIS & OMAHA RAILWAY 1880-1940	ISBN 1-882256-67-0
GREAT NORTHERN RAILWAY 1945-1970	ISBN 1-882256-56-5
MILWAUKEE ROAD 1850-1960	ISBN 1-882256-61-1
SOO LINE 1975-1992	ISBN 1-882256-68-9

TRUCKS

BEVERAGE TRUCKS 1910-1975	ISBN 1-882256-60-3
BROCKWAY TRUCKS 1948-1961	ISBN 1-882256-55-7
DODGE TRUCKS 1929-1947	ISBN 1-882256-36-0
DODGE TRUCKS 1948-1960	ISBN 1-882256-37-9
LOGGING TRUCKS 1915-1970	ISBN 1-882256-59-X
MACK® MODEL AB*	ISBN 1-882256-18-2
MACK AP SUPER DUTY TRUCKS 1926-1938*	ISBN 1-882256-54-9
MACK MODEL B 1953-1966 VOLUME 1*	ISBN 1-882256-19-0
MACK MODEL B 1953-1966 VOLUME 2*	ISBN 1-882256-34-4
MACK EB-EC-ED-EE-EF-EG-DE 1936-1951*	ISBN 1-882256-29-8
MACK EH-EJ-EM-EQ-ER-ES 1936-1950*	ISBN 1-882256-39-5
MACK FC-FCSW-NW 1936-1947*	ISBN 1-882256-28-X
MACK FG-FH-FJ-FK-FN-FP-FT-FW 1937-1950*	ISBN 1-882256-35-2
MACK LF-LH-LJ-LM-LT 1940-1956 *	ISBN 1-882256-38-7
MACK MODEL B FIRE TRUCKS 1954-1966*	ISBN 1-882256-62-X
MACK MODEL CF FIRE TRUCKS 1967-1981*	ISBN 1-882256-63-8
STUDEBAKER TRUCKS 1927-1940	ISBN 1-882256-40-9
STUDEBAKER TRUCKS 1941-1964	ISBN 1-882256-41-7

* This product is sold under license from Mack Trucks, Inc. All rights reserved.

The Iconografix Photo Archive Series is available from direct mail specialty book dealers and bookstores worldwide, or can be ordered from the publisher. For book trade and distribution information or to add your name to our mailing list contact:

Iconografix
PO Box 609/BK
Osceola, Wisconsin 54020 USA

Telephone: (715) 294-2792
(800) 289-3504 (USA)
Fax: (715) 294-3414

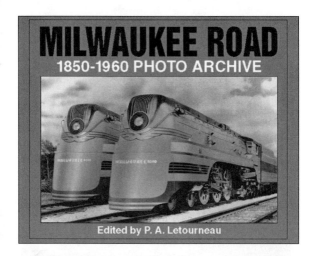

MILWAUKEE ROAD
1850-1960 PHOTO ARCHIVE
Edited by P. A. Letourneau

MORE
GREAT BOOKS FROM
ICONOGRAFIX

MILWAUKEE ROAD 1850-1960
Photo Archive ISBN 1-882256-61-1

GREAT NORTHERN RAILWAY 1945-1970
Photo Archive ISBN 1-882256-56-5

SOO LINE 1975-1992 Photo Archive
ISBN 1-882256-68-9

MACK MODEL CF FIRE TRUCKS
1967-1981 Photo Archive
ISBN 1-882256-63-8

MACK MODEL B 1953-1966 VOLUME 1
Photo Archive ISBN 1-882256-19-0

COCA-COLA: A HISTORY IN PHOTO-
GRAPHS 1930-1969 Photo Archive
ISBN 1-882256-46-8

CATERPILLAR SIXTY Photo Arhive
ISBN 1-882256-05-0

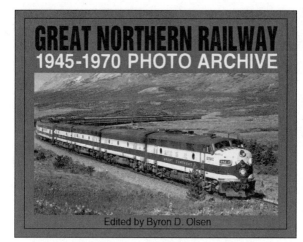

GREAT NORTHERN RAILWAY
1945-1970 PHOTO ARCHIVE
Edited by Byron D. Olsen

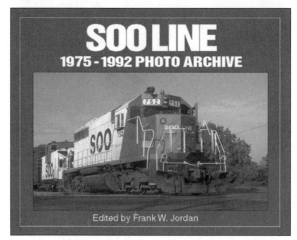

SOO LINE
1975 - 1992 PHOTO ARCHIVE
Edited by Frank W. Jordan

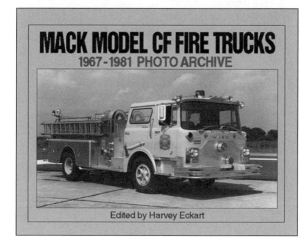

MACK MODEL CF FIRE TRUCKS
1967 - 1981 PHOTO ARCHIVE
Edited by Harvey Eckart

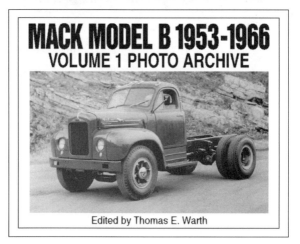

MACK MODEL B 1953-1966
VOLUME 1 PHOTO ARCHIVE
Edited by Thomas E. Warth

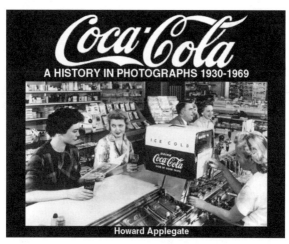

Coca-Cola
A HISTORY IN PHOTOGRAPHS 1930-1969
Howard Applegate

CATERPILLAR SIXTY
PHOTO ARCHIVE
Edited by P. A. Letourneau